Beginning

ENCOURAGEMENT AT THE START OF SOMETHING NEW

WARREN HANSON

WALDMAN HOUSE PRESS
waldmanhouse.com

This is the Beginning…

This is where

on the Wings of some new Spirit

t all will start,

with the Beat of some new Heart.

Every morning brings a Promise.   Every day has Gifts to give.

But *Today...* right *Now...* this *Minute...*

is when I begin to Live.

And the air that I am breathing
is the breeze of what could be,
as I stand here looking out
on all the things that could be Me.

And the road that goes before me,

leading somewhere out of sight,

is a brand new Opportunity

for me to get it Right.

This is the Beginning.

This is

Once upon a Time…

There are dragons to be vanquished!

There are castle walls to climb!

But this story isn't written yet.

I'm only at page One.

The Adventure that's awaiting me

has only just Begun.

There are *Mysteries* and *Treasures*.

There are daring deeds to do!

And if I speak the secret word,

then all my *Wishes* will come true.

That *Magic Word* has powers
that can make the heavens spin.
But it really is no *Secret*
that the password is…
"Begin!"

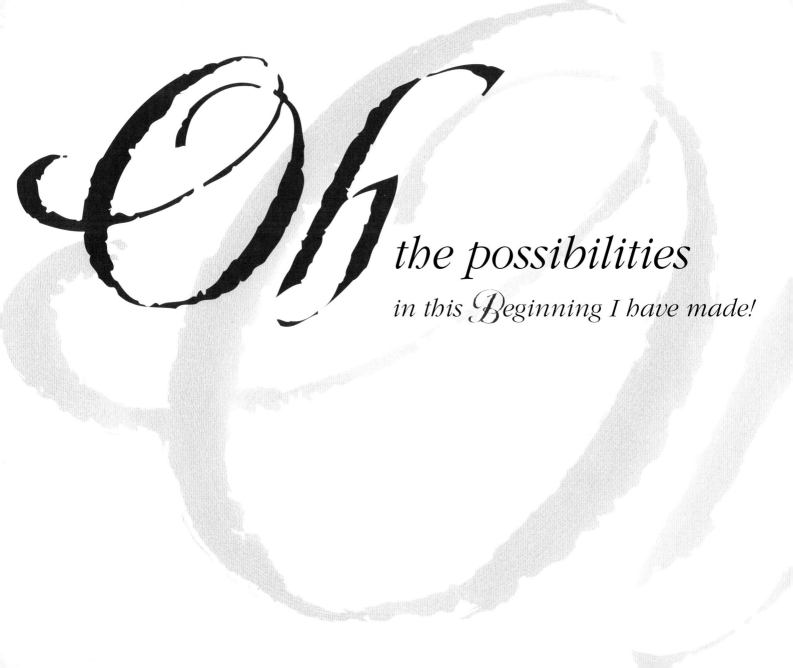

Oh the possibilities *in this Beginning I have made!*

I am Ready!...

but reluctant.

I'm Excited!...

but afraid.

Afraid that
starting
something New
leaves something
Old behind.

Afraid that
what I seek
is something
I may
Never find.

Or, if I *Find* it,

that it won't be

what I want

at all.

That what I've

left *Behind*

is what I needed

after all.

Beginning can be bittersweet,

and hard to comprehend.

It can mean that

some sweet, precious part of life

is at an End.

And the *Heart* can feel so *Hollow*

when it has to say *Good-bye*

that the thought of starting *Over*

is too *Hard* to even try.

But when I reach the *End*,

when all my days are nearly through,

I will *Not* want to look back

on all the things I *Didn't* do,

Nor regret the *Joys* and *Passions*

of the me that *Might* have been,

if *Only* I had found

the simple *Courage*

to *Begin*.

So…

This is the Beginning…

My Beginning.

My Rebirth.

I Awaken to the Wonder
of what I am Really worth.

It is a *Springtime* for the *Spirit,*

and it's *Giving me a Choice.*

So I choose to *Use* this season

as a reason to *Rejoice!*

I lift my voice in Sweet thanskgiving,

singing Loud… and not alone.

A host of Harmonies accompanies

my song of the unknown.

Loving Friends and willing Strangers,

with their voices joining in,

create a chorus of Encouragement

that begs me to Begin.

And the end?...

It's out there, Somewhere,

farther than the heart can see.

And the Power that will take me there

is Here,

inside of me.

Though there is no way I can know
how many trials I'll endure,

nor the Joys
that I may find,

there is One thing I know for sure…

This is the Beginning...